Elements
of
the
Novel

A Primer for Beginners

Elements
of
the
Novel

A Primer for Beginners

Eileen Charbonneau

2012
New Street Communications, LLC
Wickford, RI

newstreetcommunications.com

Published by New Street Communications, LLC, Wickford, RI.
newstreetcommunications.com

Contents

Introduction

by

Robert Crooke

I was immediately taken by *Elements of the Novel* and its encouraging, empowering, democratizing approach to the art and profession. There are always things a writer can learn to draw out and improve his or her talents. This guide presents an implicit understanding that even as the publishing world changes, the human capacity for telling stories, and for listening to them, is as permanent as it is universal.

Elements of *Elements* that jumped out for this novelist include: telling the stories that you like to read yourself, making the time to write, finding the living breathing elements of character and setting, and not over worrying about beginnings. Throughout, *Elements* keeps conveying how organic and alive this whole process needs to be.

All the material about drafting and revising is excellent. More than one great novelist has observed that revision *is* the art of writing. Novelist F. Scott Fitzgerald was an incredibly disciplined plotter, probably from his successful magazine writing to spec, but his greatest extended work, *The Great Gatsby*, really emerged not only in revisions but actually on the pages of the pre-publication galleys that Scribner was ready to publish. He changed many words, moved chapters around, made last minute revisions and the book went from wonderful story to brilliant and unexpected magic on the final pages … all with a blue pencil. *The Great Gatsby* was revised into life.

Mention of the market is placed in the context of putting our writing and our goals for it in proper perspective. Too many writers, especially new or developing ones, obsess far too much about selling their work before they've really learned how to write a damn novel to begin with.

Elements of the Novel gently demystifies some of the silliness and misconceptions around novel-writing that deserve to be dispelled, while it upholds and illustrates all that is good and human and artistic, even spiritual, about the enterprise. Not only is it a useful and insightful handbook for a budding or practicing novelist, but in the process, it tells a great story - Eileen Charbonneau's story - as a novelist. Bravo!

- Robert Crooke

Bridgewater, Connecticut

ROBERT CROOKE is a journalist, media executive, teacher, poet and novelist. His poetry has been published in the *The West Hills Review*, the literary journal of the Walt Whitman Birthplace on Long Island. He has lectured at Suffolk County Community College, the University of Nebraska, New York University, and the University of Connecticut. He began his career as a sports reporter and columnist for the Long Island Press and for 13 years served as North American press spokesman for Reuters, the international news group. Currently, he heads financial media relations for the US Division of Makinson Cowell, a capital markets advisory firm, founded in 1989, which provides independent research and advice to a wide range of companies based primarily in Europe and North America. His novels include *The Earth and Its Sorrows* (2010), *American Family* (2004) and *Sunrise* (2007). He and his wife reside in Bridgewater, Connecticut.

First edition, 1973.

Ever since wearing out three copies of Strunk and White's magnificent The Elements of Style, *I've wondered: Is it possible to write such a brilliant distillation for the novel writing process? I wonder no longer. It isn't. But this is the result of my effort.* **- Eileen Charbonneau**

Great things are not done by impulse, but by a series of small things brought together. **- Vincent Van Gogh**

Preface

Why do writers write? Because it isn't there. **- Thomas Berger**

What is a good novel? It is compelling characters in a good, galloping plot, well told.

This is what everything in this guide aspires to be: simple, but not easy.

Writing is a craft. Writers work hard to master the elements of their craft. They read, they learn from other good writers. They write letters, use the Internet, they try many genres of writing.

Creative writing is an art. Artists are sensitive - they use and explore all their senses. They know how to think and develop ideas. They are on the alert always. They are seldom bored because everything is fodder for story.

Backstory

This guide is based on my over thirty years at the craft.

My path began in a stormy winter in Buffalo, New York. I was a recent college graduate, in deep love with my new husband and beautiful baby and absorbed in learning how to be a good wife and mom. The last thing on my mind was more schooling. But my friend Karen saw me as isolated. She thought I wrote beautiful letters so why not learn more about what I might do with this gift? She dragged me into an adult education night class at a local college entitled "How To Write Articles For Pleasure and Profit." (Most adult-ed classes were "for pleasure and profit" at the time - bad economy!)

That class and its teacher, Diana Gleasner, were life changers. Diana was the first person I'd ever met who made her living as a writer. I had the notion that writers were rarefied beings who were much more learned than I would ever be, and lived in ivory towers when they weren't running with the bulls or on safari. Diana looked like, well … me! She had the beautiful glow of someone who had found her calling.

Diana Gleasner was a kind, encouraging and gifted teacher to a very fledgling writer, who could not even define if the vignettes she was handing in about interesting people she had met were fiction or non-fiction. (They were both. Even then, I was on the road to becoming a novelist!)

I certainly did not have many elements mastered by the end of Diana's class, but I did have a strong desire to learn and master them. And I had this wonderful woman's permission to call myself a writer. "Writers write," she told us. "You write. Of course you're writers."

By the end of the year, I had sold my first article. I was a professional writer. When I cashed that check, I saw a way I might be able to work my long, long journey from home base, so that I could be a full time parent to my children.

Since that Buffalo winter, I've had wonderful teachers, editors and advocates. I've also had the privilege of teaching many gifted and hard-working writers.

In recent years, I have taught day-long seminars at Scott Meyer's wonderful independent bookstore Merritt Books in Millbrook, New York. It's here the elements of *Elements of the Novel* have been developing. We take a couple of elements at each session and explore, discuss and write exercises based in them. Our goal is for deeper understanding and mastery. I am so grateful to my fellow novelists who have shared their works in progress and helped me develop this program.

Have you felt lost inside the world of your novel? Perhaps stumped about whether or not a scene is advancing your plot? Or if a run of dialogue truly illuminates the characters speaking it? Try going to the element that's giving you grief and play there. Try one of the exercises suggested. It is my hope that this book may offer you a new perspective that leads to deeper, more compelling storytelling.

Why Write?

If you do not breathe through writing, if you do not cry out in writing, or sing in writing, then don't write, because our culture has no use for it - **Anais Nin**

There are lots of good answers to the question: *Why write?* At the core is desire. Do you like to write? Do you enjoy the process?

I am not of the "open a vein" school. The genesis of this idea is usually attributed to beloved sportswriter Red Smith as: "There's nothing to writing. All you do is sit down at a typewriter and open a vein." Hey, didn't anybody ever tell Red that there's no crying in baseball?

Don't get me wrong. Writing is hard, hard work. For me it's right up there with my other calling - parenting ... the hardest work I've ever loved.

I find great joy in every part of the process. Well okay, maybe not the spelling.

So I hope the big question you ask yourself is: *Am I called to write?*

And why write novels?

Now, why do you want to write novels? In my view, there is only one correct answer to this question: *That you can't NOT write them.*

truth and Truth

"If there's a book you really want to read, but it hasn't been written yet, then you must write it." - **Toni Morrison**

Want to tell the truth, deal with facts and opinion? That's what journalists and biographers and essayists do. That's the land of who/what/when/how non-fiction. It's about telling the truth.

Fiction is about telling *The Truth*. And that's the land of the whys.

Tell Me a Story ...

If you are a twenty-first century novelist, here's the good news and the bad news. The bad news is that writing a good novel is hard work in interesting publishing times ... and I mean "interesting" as in Bugs Bunny at the beauty shop nervously filing the nails of the great hairy creature while saying that monsters are the most *INteresting* people.

The good news is that it's a forgiving form. Unlike poetry or a children's picture book, every single word is not crucial to the success of the whole. You can get away with a clunker or two, a minor character that leans toward caricature, a weak transition, as long as the cumulative effect is still a wonderful journey that is worth your reader's hard-earned money and time.

More good news: My friend and wonderful novelist Juilene Osborne-McKnight is fond of saying that human beings are hot-wired for story. Even in these times of free downloads and closing booksellers, of publishers still scrambling into the 21st century, of writers pondering questions like: are social media sites the new slush pile? ... our need to tell each other stories is not going anywhere

Still more good news: You are writing in English, a language that is rich in vocabulary deposited on that tiny island by a whole host of invading and invaded peoples. From Latin to French to Germanic to the four corners of the earth, it's a goulash (from Hungary) galore (Gaelic)! Thanks to the two main streams of head-based (Latin) and emotion-based (Anglo-Saxon), it's why we can be both bellicose and warlike, have women and ladies, females and damsels, girls and gals.

The glory (and the danger) comes in the choosing.

As Mark Twain wrote: "The difference between the right word and the almost right word is the difference between lightning and lightning bug."

If you were writing in French or German or Italian, you'd have to clutter up your sentences with adverbs and adjectives to do the work that a verb like "saunter" does. Oh, the verbs! Do we have them and are they strong! Even their tenses are strong (drink, drank, drunk). Those ham and eggs on your breakfast plate? The chicken is *involved*. The pig is *committed*.

Yet more good news: I am firm in the belief that writing is a cumulative art. The more you do it, the better you get at it.

It's Elemental

So you've got a great, precise and rich language to work with. And you've got the elements broken down in this guide. As in Chemistry (which I never studied in school and am sure I would have failed miserably if I had ... but I can *imagine* its principles!) each contributes to the life of your novel.

The best novels have strong elements. Some you're likely more inclined toward ... be it description, dialogue or characterization. Others you may have to work harder to attain.

Elements can do triple duty. Test your elements using the three parts of a good novel. Pull out a narrative tool, say, a dialogue exchange. Test it. Does this dialogue move the plot? Does it illuminate character? Is it well told? All three? Well done!

The Exercises

We learn in varied and wondrous ways. Learning enters through
the ear, through the eye, and through the hand. Which way do you
learn best?

For some, learning comes best through the ear ... those great
listeners who absorb a well crafted lecture and are on fire with
knowledge thereafter.

For others, sight works better. These learners love flowcharts and
diagrammed sentences, timelines and re-enactments. And they
devour how-to books!

Others learn best through the hand. From the earliest age it was all
about, "ME do it, Mama!" Those might enjoy the exercises at the
end of chapters the best.

No matter our preference, we all learn in all three ways. So I
encourage all readers of this guide to try some of the exercises.
They are based on the ones that have been most successful in my
seminars. Most of them only take five minutes each. In my
seminars, we work on them, then read the results out loud. Our
goal is to become illuminated about each others' work and our

process. These little assignments are intended to imaginatively exercise our writing muscles.

Good writers read, write and share (talk and listen) with other good writers and readers. I wish for you a learning experience that is complex and rich.

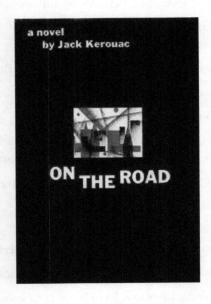

First edition, 1957.

I

Process

All writers have it. It varies with the individual. It's flexible with life circumstances. It's how we get things done. It's process.

Part 1: Time

The first element of the writing process is *time*.

Lots of people would love to have written a novel. Novelists write novels. This requires writing. Writing requires time.

Novelists don't find time; they make it. I've had writer friends who put on the writing harness and work twelve hour days for six weeks to get a first draft done. Others carve out two hours a day. Others, four hours over a weekend. There are many stories of novelists who have made time in waiting rooms, on the sidelines at soccer practice or in the dead of night to get the book done.

Of course active thinking about your story can be done anytime ... but do pay attention to basic safety rules on the road and when your child's solo comes up at that school concert!

If you establish a regular time and place to write, and get yourself there seven times, it will become a habit - and a good one. You'll be in gear when that time and place rolls along. You'll make yourself hot-wired for it, I promise.

Lark, Owl, or Stiff?

If you're lucky enough to choose your writing time, you'll probably notice that you're better at certain times of the day. Most writers I know are Larks, Owls or Stiffs.

I'm a Lark; the creative energy flows better in early morning. I get another spurt in the afternoon, so that's when I usually do my research. Others are Owls; late night is their time to write most productively. Still others are working Stiffs; they hum along on an eight hour, nine to five day.

When your own creative energy flows best is a good thing to know about yourself.

Distractions

One of the nice things about being a Lark or an Owl writer is that there tend to be fewer distractions from the outside world in those hours ... the phone ringing, the meal to be prepared, the scraped knee of a child.

But the Internet and its labyrinth of pleasures and distractions looms 24/7, and it's right there, a keystroke away. Resist!

Part 2: Product

The second element of the writing process is, well ... writing. Yes, committing the words to the page on that screen. Fill it up. One word leads to another. Sentences form, then paragraphs, then chapters. When you write THE END you have a novel. It's that simple.

Not easy, but simple.

Plotter or Panster?

The terms "plotter" and "panster" seem to have their origins in genre writing land. They are useful in describing what kind of novelist you are.

Before writing the novel, the writer who devises a strictly-adhered-to outline is a plotter.

The novelist who writes her story from the seat of her pants, letting her mind stream along, is a *pantster*.

One sounds anal, overflowing with charts, maps, character profiles and timelines, right?

And the other? A dithering slacker, going down all sorts of rabbit holes on the way to a perhaps less-than-coherent novel.

In reality few novelists are pure plotters or pantsters.

But it's useful to discover which best describes you.

I am basically a pantster. Before I begin, I know the main characters I want to journey with, and I know how I'd like it to end, and that's about it.

For my novel *Waltzing in Ragtime* I knew I wanted to write about a forest ranger in the early twentieth century history of the National Parks. I knew he was a good son and father, and had a lot of physical courage. Matthew Hart wasn't afraid of anything ... except earthquakes. And I knew by my novel's end he needed to be living in San Francisco on April 18, 1906, on the morning of The Big One.

But, as an historical novelist, I spend a lot of time before beginning my novels researching time and place. In this I would seem more of a plotter, with timelines featuring historic events, customs, even foods that may inform my plot at the ready. This stimulates ideas about the character and narrative information I have in mind. I continue to research throughout my drafts, as gaps and questions come up.

My novels tend to build themselves through many drafts. This may be the result of my not knowing very much about the middle.

I once swallowed the nonsense that pansters are undisciplined louts, and thought that perhaps my novels wouldn't take so long to write if I tried to be more of a plotter. So I took an idea for a book, wrote index cards with every scene and what happens in it all worked out.

The result? Disaster! I never wrote the novel, because I knew too much and lost interest. I went back to my pantster ways, which get the book done.

I doubt that the time element is an issue for either method. When the plotter writes *The End*, I'm sure she's happy that she took time and effort and that her structured plan produced results. And when the pantster gets there, she's happy that although she had to throw out that beautiful scene when she explored another plot possibility, she arrived at the same place.

And both novelists have served her story.

Does your story come out of plot or out of character? That may help you understand what method to use. If plot is the driving force and your characters exist to serve it, then pre-writing, storyboarding and timelines may be your friend.

If you are a panster, your characters may start out looking like someone you know or sharing a trait of forgetfulness like Uncle Warren or bossyness like your Aunt Meg. But then things start happening as you put them in your story. They change. They even talk back to you when you give them the wrong thing to say or do.

In an essay in the *Newsweek* of September 26, 2011, novelist Nicholas Sparks wrote about how he knows his needs before he begins a book. They are four: to know how the characters meet, to know what's driving the story, to understand the conflict, and to know how the story will end.

What do YOU need?

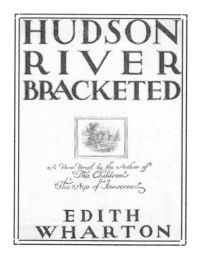

First edition, 1929.

First edition, 1958.

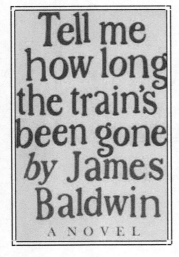

First edition, 1968.

2

Structure

Draw your chair up close to the edge of the precipice ... and I'll tell you a story.
- F. Scott Fitzgerald

Every novel, even the most experimental, has a structure. Both plotters and pantsters need one, although at different times during each's process.

Successful storytellers have always crafted their tales. Aristotle wrote about the *Three Act Structure*, based on the epic poem. Both wonderful teachers and blood-sucking shysters before and after him have drawn charts and crafted building blocks and computer software programs that present tried and true formulas about structure.

If you need one of those complicated things, search elsewhere.

Structure is, for me, one of those not easy, but simple elements.

It's based on every time you are asked what your book is about. To wit: First you tell how your story starts. Then you tell what happens next, then after that, then after that. Until you say how it ends

That's right: every novel has a BEGINNING, a MIDDLE and an END.

If you're a plotter, your structure, broken down into its parts, creates the outline of your novel. If you're a pantster, it will guide your revisions.

In each part of your novel, things should happen. So, one at a time:

First edition, 1952.

The Beginning

Bring all your intelligence to bear on your beginning.

- Elizabeth Bowen

Here's the Prime Directive of *The Beginning*: To hold the promise of the rest of your novel: the promise of being worth your reader's time and the engagement of her attention and imagination.

Biggest problem with the beginning? Finding it. So my suggestion is: don't mess too much with the beginning until at least after the first draft of the whole book is written. To do anything otherwise is to invite the madness of endlessly rewriting before you've half begun.

It's got to start somewhere. Plunge on in at a place that interests you. (Oh, sorry, plotter. For you: at that place you've determined by your outline, is the beginning of your story.)

Okay, now finish writing your book.

I'll wait. Done? Great, now let's take another look at your beginning.

Does your beginning introduce your story, your characters and establish the dramatic premise: what the major conflicts are?

Does your beginning give at least a hint as to what kind of story you're telling, be it Science Fiction, Fantasy, Romance, Mystery?

Does it plant the reader firmly in its setting time and place?

Does it contain conflict?

Does it set your tone and style?

Does it show your choice of viewpoint?

And, always, always, always: Is it essential?

The Beginning as HOOK

T.S. Eliot wrote: "If you start with a bang, you won't end with a whimper."

The beginnings of my novels are the places where I tend to rewrite the most, because the beginning is also your hook, your selling tool to both the reader (yes, this is going to be worth your time, dear reader) and your publisher (yes, this is worth investing in, dear publisher). For your publisher the time to do this seems to be getting shorter and shorter, so I consider the first 50 pages important, the first chapter more important and the first page most important for this purpose.

The Middle

The *middle*, of course, joins the *beginning* to the *end* of your story. But it's much more. It's your chance to explore the elements of your novel - setting, character, conflicts. And plot, plot, plot: what happens next? And then what? Every event of the middle should serve to move the plot forward. If it also illuminates character and expresses your theme...you're cooking with gas. But strive for at least two of the three.

Here's the Prime Directive of *The Middle*: To deepen and expand your story without losing its pace.

Biggest Problem of Middles: Sagging

If you tend to lounge around in your middle, as I do, this involves cutting. Two wonderful scenes that accomplish the same purpose? One of them has to go. Two characters who are sounding alike and serving the same purpose? Oops. Combine them, or kill one. Does a scene slow down the pace ... not vary it, but slow it down? It needs to be shortened or cut.

The End

Have you written those words: *The End* on the last page of your manuscript? Congratulations! Most people who begin a novel don't get there.

Okay, back to work.

Here's the Prime Directive of *The End*: To resolve and satisfy while seeming inevitable.

Your ending must deliver on the promise within the rest of the novel.

In some genres, the readers expect a certain ending. Romance readers want love to conquer all. Mystery readers want that crime solved. Disappoint them at your peril!

Getting the ending just right is a craft and an art. Give it your time and attention. You want the reader satisfied, but also hungry to read your next book. You want your characters to live on in your reader's mind.

Questions should be answered, all secrets revealed, unless your novel is part of a series. Then your ending should be satisfying, with just enough hidden to bring back the reader for part two or six or fifteen.

Ways to Work on Your Ending

Go all *Hollywood* and test it out on audiences for feedback.

Another Hollywood trick: alternative endings ... see which one seems *True*.

Make sure it is not based on *Deus Ex Machina* ... no goddess descending in her chariot to tie up loose ends, no cavalry rat-tat-tatting in to save the day (or add to the decimation of your people, if you're Native American). Have your characters resolve all those plot points you've worked so hard developing throughout your story.

End of The End

Just as your book's first sentence should be carefully crafted, so should your last.

At the end of my own *Waltzing in Ragtime*, after slogging through all the heat and fire aftermath of the 1906 San Francisco earthquake, it felt good to write: "Then, with neither lightning nor thunder as a warning, it began to rain."

Diana Gabaldon's *Outlander* ending line is perfect for this first book in her famous series: leaving open a wide range of promise for her next volume:

"And the world was all around us, new with possibility."

So ... As Diana advises (and she took her own advice, didn't she? Ahh, sagas!): What are you waiting for? Go start another.

*

If you write one story, it may be bad; if you write a hundred, you have the odds in your favor. **- Edgar Rice Burroughs**

First edition, 1977.

3

Setting

Where?

Think about it. The essential obligation of the novelist is to take her reader somewhere, isn't it?

Setting is vital. Setting is a constant. We are always in a particular place at a particular time. In the same way, setting should be a living, breathing element on every page of your novel.

Place is sensory. Think of the novels of Tony Hillerman. The American Southwest locations of detectives Joe Leaphorn and Jim Chee are so vivid they are often described by critics as another character, a living being. How did Hillerman do this? Methodically. He made sure there were at least two expressions of his characters experiencing their setting through their senses on each page.

So, what smells are wafting up from that neighborhood stoop in Brooklyn on your April day in 1924?

How neatly are the beds made in that army barracks?

Is the music familiar or discordant as a character steps into that speakeasy?

What does the room's wall of gilt-framed awards say about that cinematographer?

Who is experiencing the setting?

Places can be observed objectively or subjectively, depending on each scene's point of view. If you choose a subjective point of view, you can use your setting to illuminate character.

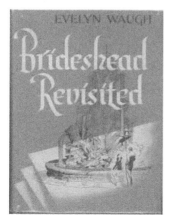

First U.S. edition, 1946.

The Passion of Place

Try describing a place you love or hate. The writing will have life!
The settings of your novel should be full of such places, brimming
with life and feeling.

In *Bleak House*, Charles Dickens describes a London November
with " ... Smoke lowering down from chimney-pots, making a soft
black drizzle, with flakes of soot in it as big as full-grown
snowflakes - gone into mourning, one might imagine, for the death
of the sun."

Even from that distant, "one might imagine" viewpoint, the
description dazzles with its passion!

What can you do with a convict breathing the air of freedom
outside the prison walls? Or the feel of the swamp water, the sound
of shotgun fire or the baying of hounds on the trail of his escape?
How can you put us there?

Details

How important are the details of your place? The writer who accumulates details is communicating something different form the one who chooses carefully and specifically to illuminate place.

When you travel to a new setting, do you enjoy writing about the new place on the spot? Or do you prefer to write from memory, knowing that what's important will be filtered through the time away?

How Much is Too Much?

Don't assume your readers will know where you are, if you merely say "street" or "farm house." But paragraphs of description leading off every change of scene will probably bog down the momentum of your story. The right balance can be struck. Good description of setting is embedded and essential. If your description can do double or triple duty, you're cooking.

Exercises

1. Observe a place, TAKE us there. Objective or subjective, real or imaginary, but be aware of your choices. Fueled by passion ... place you LOVE or HATE the most. Use your senses.

2. Now, change that place's genre. Make it so your reader knows within moments that it is a setting for a mystery novel, or a Western, a Fantasy, or Horror.

3. Go through each new setting of your novel. Make sure you have used at least two senses in describing it.

4. Try writing a place from your novel using only one sense, or one sense at a time. Have you learned something new?

5. Try the cinematic trick of describing landscape in long shot, then medium shot, then close up detail as a way to establish place.

4

Research

A man will turn over half a library to make one book. - **Samuel Johnson**

And so should you! Every novel needs research, whether it's set in the past, present or future, whether you take your readers to a Federal era plantation in Virginia, the teeming streets of Manhattan in World War II, or your memories of last month. Good research provides your story with accuracy: the projection of a bullet, the symptoms of a disease, the workings of the heart.

Why

Authenticity. That's what every novel should have, and that's what research can help you achieve.

It may be based in a closer observation of what you know. If you're writing about a family struggling to stay in the middle class, pay close attention to your grocery and gas, and heating bills - fluctuations might send the bread winner to her credit cards to provide necessities.

It may be a grounded guide that helps your imagination take flight. So, if we did find a way to travel faster than the speed of light. ... Or, what might be a life circumstance needed for a slave owner's son *not* to view field workers as his father's property?

When

When to research? Before, during and after the progress of your novel.

Let your initial research help with the foundation of your plot and characterization. How long should this initial phase last? Until you have a feel for your setting. Some novelists get lost or overwhelmed here. I've known gifted storytellers who get stuck *ala*: "One more book about the table manners of eighteenth century Virginia and I'll be ready to start." Yes, that's TOO long! You are a storyteller, not a scholar. You don't have to know everything. You need to know the things that serve your story.

When you are in your draft process and come upon something you don't know you can either stop and look it up (how long IS the time from which you've been bitten by a rabid animal before you know you've been infected?) or make a note and keep writing. Try not to take too much time from your writing process.

Once you're editing, the results of your research may change the course of your novel. Don't worry, you'll make it work. And that research will make your story stronger and more authentic.

After your novel is complete, your first readers may catch some points that don't sound right. When I was working with my editor, the great Sandra Jordan on my first published novel *The Ghosts of Stony Clove*, she noticed a scene where I had my young heroine Ginny offering a bowl of red raspberries to her friend Asher, who has just returned home from a sojourn in the American West.

I loved the scene and the raspberries part in it. It was one of those triple duty moments. It exposed character: the way Asher ate the berries showed he was the still-always-hungry-kid who'd left four years before. It also moved the plot as Ginny realizes she'd better get him to the next scene: her mother's place for a good meal. And it worked on a symbolic level - since red raspberries are part of the rose family, she was offering him more than food, she was offering him love.

The problem? Sandra said she didn't think raspberries would be growing wild in New York's Hudson Valley in October. Well, I went berry picking with my family every Fall and so I knew they did! Still, she asked me to double check. A call to the farm where we enjoyed our berry picking proved Sandra quite right ... the berries we were picking were an eleven year-old hybrid strain, bred specifically for leaf-peeping tourists to enjoy! Not available to Ginny Rockwell in the autumn of 1807!

What did I do? Change the fruit to hearty wild blackberries - content with hitting two out of the magic three goals.

Side note: When I tell that story to adults, they are suitably impressed with Sandra's and my diligence. But when I tell it to young people, their eyes glow. They say things like: "You do all that, just for us kids? Wow!" This reminds me what a privilege it is to write for young people and how they deserve our very best.

Where

Research both takes you out of your novel and feeds it. Sources for research include the Internet, libraries, experts and bookstores. When I'm plunging into one of my historical novels, I like to explore well-written children's books on the era first. They tend to be written clearly and with the big picture and ideas up front. I go back to children's non-fiction for specifics too - from how sailors tie knots to what life was like for a family living near Civil War battlefields.

Movies and the Internet

I put these two together because they are both handy and fun. But they are also starting points.

You may be inspired when you see a great fictional account of the life of Mozart's sister. (Hmmm, I wonder if Chopin had a sister?) From there you might head to the Internet, to find out life specifics of dear Nannerl Mozart, and see where the screenwriter took liberties. You're ten websites deep now, and deep in a hot-headed debate (Dad was a monster or a devoted guide, little brother was a selfish brat ... no he wasn't, he stuck up for his sister and her marriage choice ...) Need more facts! Find *.edu* and *.gov* sites for scholars. They cite biographies that go back through the centuries to accounts by contemporaries. Before you know it, you have just made a trip to Salzburg and touched Nannerl's harpsichord keys. And yes, it all started with an afternoon at the movies!

Interviews

Most experts and aficionados are most happy to share the fruits of their study. Come prepared with good questions. Take good notes and enjoy their passion for their subject. Say thank you, in person, and on the acknowledgement page of your novel.

Libraries

Make friends with librarians, and those wonderful brimming-with-knowledge places. State libraries, university libraries, genealogy collections. Support them. Join all libraries that you can. Find out what's available at local historical societies. Most libraries are part of wider systems and allow searches from home on your computer. Use inter-library loans to save travel time and the planet.

Local History

Even the smallest communities have repositories of their own history. Was this town the center of the precision machine tool industry of the 1930s? Was it home to a folklorist who preserved the ancient ballads of its first settlers? How did it nurture those lads who were always tinkering with bicycles and flying machines?

Tours of local homes can yield great tidbits of information, sometimes preserved in booklets available in the gift shop.

Up To Date

Make sure your sources present what is latest known on your subject. New theories on everything abound, from the origin of the human species to time travel. If it's controversial, you may have to choose a side, whether it's the latest ways to deal with Asperger's, osteoporosis, climate change, or a misbehaving child.

Record the Source

Wherever you find that revelation or tidbit, record your sources.
You may need more detail later. You may have to check and
double check when challenged by a reader or editor. You've done
the work, enjoy the security.

Travel

Yes, go to the settings of your novel if you can. Yes, I have just
given you permission to make a grand tour of all of Bavarian King
Ludwig II's magnificent castles! Even if it's your own home town,
visit it anew, as a researcher. See it as your characters do.

For my novel *Watch Over Me*, set in World War II, I enjoyed my
research in New York City. It was not the city I knew well, but the
one of another generation. I re-visited immigrant neighborhoods
and imagined other languages being spoken around me, other
cooking scents in the air. I found remnants of The Automat,
Central Park's Sheep Meadow when it actually had sheep grazing,
and Coney Island wonders long since burned to the ground.

Imagination Stations

How about researching a fantasy novel, or other speculative fiction? I tell my imaginative students of all ages: what you are writing is real because it exists in your imagination. Great, freeing, liberating, right? But with liberty comes responsibility!

The fantasy and sci-fi writers call it "world building" and it must have its own rules and make sense, whether it's why YOUR vampire goes sunbathing or how people cope with living on that world with the seven moons wreaking havoc on the tides.

Many fantasy novels draw on an historical time period, be it Greek city states or Victorian or Steampunk or mythology from the Celts or folklore of the Gypsies. Your research should start there.

Whatever world you build, keep working on making all the Whys make sense down to the smallest details.

Oops

We so revere the written word that we sometimes forget a person can lie just as easily on paper as by spoken word. Check, double check and triple check your many sources. Keep them up to date. Knowledge is constantly changing. New information and artifacts come to light. History gets re-interpreted. Old or new sources are granted legitimacy.

I often write about Native American cultures. Most of them have no written history and rely on storytelling traditions. I'm happy to say that respect for these sources has risen in recent years. But in the past a how-we-got-here story or a why-we-do-things-this-way was dismissed or corrupted by misunderstanding interpretations. And these misunderstandings have been perpetuated until we're left with stereotypes and caricatures of America's first peoples. I am most grateful for the trust that clan elders have honored me with.

In the End ...

Your novel is the work of your imagination. You have no set obligation towards the truth, only the Truth. You can put Edgar Allan Poe on the moon, the way Isaac Asimov did, or research until you find out that Thomas Jefferson was actually on that road in Virginia in 1816 and may indeed have met up with your fictional character. Literal-minded critics may have problems with your choices, no matter how conservative or liberal your imagination. Have your poetic license handy to flash at them.

First edition, 1985.

First edition, 1974.

5

Character

Begin with an individual, and before you know it you have created a type; begin with a type, and you find you have created -- nothing. **- F. Scott Fitzgerald**

The living, breathing heart of your novel lies within its characters. Your reader must care enough about them and what they are doing, to spend that precious commodity, time, with them.

For me, the writing of a novel is a voyage of discovering character. By the end, characters are old friends. They have changed; so have I.

Constructing Character

Like their real counterparts, the characters in your novel exist in many layers. They have physical dimensions. Your character is just-so high; he weighs just-so much. He may have health problems ... a hunched back, a constant cold. How does he walk? How free or tight is his smile?

Your characters also exist on a sociological level. Where were they born? Did they have their parents' love as children? Who are their friends? Are they affluent, middle class, or poor?

Add to the physical and social aspects your characters' psychological states. What are their basic temperaments? Are they resigned to outside fates, or eager to meet life's challenges? What are their goals, fears, disappointments, frustrations?

And the character/plot link: What does your character need? To survive in the Arctic wilderness? To find a brother? Or his murderer? To get home?

Revealing Character

Ray Bradbury wrote: "First, find out what your hero wants, then follow him."

There are many ways to show character. If you are using one of the intimate points of view, you are revealing the whole plot through one character's eyes. But whatever way you tell your story, you are never limited in ways to reveal character. You can reveal through the narrative, but also by what your characters say and what they do. And then there's what other characters do with them, and say about them.

Place

With what does your character surround herself? What does her bedroom look like? What books are on the reading table?

Plot

How does your characters interact with the plot? What is she like in action?

Other Characters

Interaction is a great way to bring out character. Others love, hate, are exasperated by your character, which reveals the character of both.

Dialogue

Other characters speak of your character. And she speaks for herself.

Backstory

Your characters have lived before the time frame of your novel. You can illuminate character through memories, contrast, and objects from the characters' pasts.

Exercises

1. Pull one of your characters from a scene. Now describe her in detail from her toes up to her head. How can you pull elements of this to illuminate character?

2. Outside/Inside portraits. Take one of your characters and write a description of him objectively. Then switch to first person and have him tell you how he sees himself.

3. Exaggeration: This is an exercise that works well for actors too. It is fun and loosening to exaggerate a character description. Try

comparing a character to an animal, or who looks delicious, or who is the embodiment of evil or greed or humor. Something interesting and illuminating might well pop out.

First edition, 1984.

6

Point Of View (P.O.V.)

Who is telling your story?

That's one of the first questions a novelist asks, isn't it? Yet point of view issues can bedevil writers all the way through the final drafts, because the story changes depending on who is telling it.

Some say the point of view in fiction determines whose eyes the reader experiences the story through. That may not be precise enough. It also mixes POV with Voice. The author is telling the story, of course. It's her voice that will come through, consciously or unconsciously. But throughout the story the "camera" lens has a viewpoint. Sometimes it's in the sky. Sometimes it's on a character's shoulder. That's viewpoint.

There are many choices. Each comes with different problems, responsibilities and effects.

Imagine a traffic accident with nine people involved:

The drivers, four pedestrians, a police officer, a passerby with her cell-phone camera, and the pilot of a helicopter overhead.

Now, imagine each telling the story of what was seen, heard, felt and experienced in the moments before, during, and after the accident. Those are the choices you are facing when writing your novel.

The three categories are first, second and third person. Each comes with variations. Then there's God: all-knowing, all-seeing, omniscient.

Some novelists are known for their mastery of one point of view, and work in it exclusively. Some genres lend themselves to one or two. Some novelists mix several within one story.

The First Person P.O.V.

The first person is telling the story from the "I" viewpoint. This can be the main character. It can also be a less important witness character. Or even a re-teller: a person telling the story that she was told by someone else.

When the "I" is intimate, and a main character, it can lend a sense of closeness for the reader. Think of Scout imparting the events of *To Kill A Mockingbird*.

The first person viewpoint is often used in young adult novels and mysteries.

Why and Why Now?

When in first person, it's important for the writer to know how the story is being told. Is the viewpoint character writing it down? Is she telling it out loud? Is she thinking it to herself? Is it meant to be read or is it a private diary? How much time has gone by since the events of the story? Why is the story being told now?

I opened my YA novel *The Ghosts of Stony Clove* with my storyteller, Ginny, writing the first pages of a diary that was given to her by another character to keep her in bed, although she's not ill. By the end the reader knows why she's there.

The way your first person narrator is writing the story will affect how you write it.

As intimate as it is, first person is also limiting. If your narrator was not on hand for crucial parts of the story, how do you tell them? I make sure there are good storytellers on hand. There is a four year separation between Ginny and Asher in *The Ghosts of Stony Clove*. When Asher returns he's got a tale to tell and a good listener in Ginny.

Second Person P.O.V.

The second person point of view is when the narrator addresses either himself (sometimes a younger version of himself), another character, or the reader as "you." It's important to establish who the "you" is. This choice of storytelling can be effective in getting the reader to trust the teller and accept the story. It can be visceral, especially when the reader is the "you." Think of the *Choose Your Own Adventure* books some of us read when we were ten. And gaming narratives.

But although novelists as far back as Tolstoy and Hawthorne have used the second person POV in sections of novels, and more current storytellers like Tom Robbins (1994's *Half Asleep in Frog Pajamas*) and Tim O'Brien (1990's *The Things They Carried*), it remains a more likely choice for short story and non-fiction works like cookbooks and self help guides. Why? It tends to be difficult to sustain. And directive. And preachy. Like this book.

Third Person P.O.V.

In the third person point of view, the viewpoint characters are referred to as "he" and "she" and the narrator is not a character in the story.

Here are some third person viewpoint variations:

The third person omniscient narrator knows everything - the thoughts, feelings, and actions of all characters - and can relate whatever the writer chooses.

More limited is the third person objective, where the narrator can only relate what is seen and heard ... just the facts, ma'am.

While within the third person limited, the narrator is only able to see into the mind and heart of a single character in whose viewpoint the narrator resides.

In a genre like Romance, third person limited within the lovers' points of view can be very effective. The readers of Romance novels are going to be most heavily invested in the hearts and minds of these two.

Whose Head is It, Anyway?

Viewpoint is a vital part of characterization. It is a great way to get to know and study your characters. Do this, and your narrative will be stronger. Perception is part of who your characters are, so think about how your viewpoint character perceives the world.

My novel *The Randolph Legacy* is told in part through Ethan Randolph's point of view. His perception is marked by his unusual experience - he has spent half his young life as a prisoner of war aboard a British Man of War. This has made him both childlike and cynical, with great gaps in his experience, but with a quick survivor's wit. He's spent many years in darkness, so he has a keenly developed sense of smell. He uses all to understand his new environments in the outside world.

How does your viewpoint character perceive the world? It will be marked by profession (an artist will see the scene differently than a banker will). It will be marked by what she values, by what she thinks important. What's her emotional state? What's her investment in what's about to happen? What's her relationship to the other characters in the scene? What's her dominant sense?

Head-Hopping

The biggest problem with point of view? Head-Hopping.

When the reader is riding along inside the head of one of your characters, she can experience all five senses while there. It takes effort to pack it all up and move into another character's head. It can be disorienting for the reader.

How much is too much?

The simple rule is to choose one character and follow an entire scene through her eyes only. It is most often a character who is at the heart of the action.

If you're changing perspective, ask yourself what the story gains by you doing so at this moment.

Should your P.O.V. character be an observer, or an active participant? What insights does your character have on what is happening?

Choice of point of view changes and illuminates your story.

Voice

Voice is the attitude of the writer towards her story. If you're writing in first person, the narrator's voice is the voice of the novel. Think of Scout in *To Kill A Mockingbird*, Stephanie Plum in *One For The Money* and its sequels. Narrative voice is part of how your story is told. It's what suits that story. Voice comes through in manner, word choice, dialect.

Some novelists have real "thumbprints" of a voice. Raymond Chandler, Jane Austin, Arthur Conan Doyle. Other novelists disappear behind the voice of a main character, and that's the voice we remember.

Exercises

Finding the right point of view and voice for your novel may come easily as the narrative evolves. For some writers it is instinctual, but most of us bumble along before hitting our stride.

1. If a scene doesn't seem to be working, try changing viewpoints and seeing if another one may be more effective. If you're struggling with character or motivation, this can help too. Instead of narrating the scene from a main character's point of view, try switching to an observer, or the antagonist. One of the most

powerful things I was taught: in your antagonist's point of view, he or she is the hero of the story. Explore that viewpoint and find out why. The switch may not hold in your novel, but seeing the narrative unfolding through another set of eyes may make a character more clear or a thread of plot tie in.

2. Who are your viewpoint characters? Learn more about them by asking what they notice first in a new environment? What is their dominant sense? Are they optimistic? Interested in the world? Politics? Culture? Children? Are they sentimental? Trusting? Trustworthy?

Now, are their perception and temperament coming through the viewpoint of their scenes?

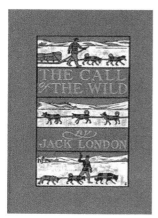

First edition, 1903.

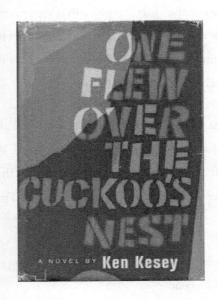

First edition, 1962.

7

Drafting

Put down everything that comes into your head and then you're a writer. But an author is one who can judge his own stuff's worth, without pity, and destroy most of it. - **Colette**

Is it drafty in here? Well, it's about time. We've covered the discovery phase of your novel - making time, doing your research, establishing your setting and characters, and discovering viewpoint. It's time for the three draft process that I call Sound, Sense and Sing.

DRAFT 1: *Sound*

Turn all editors off and write your story. There's a blank page or screen. You need to fill it. Keep filling it until the scene is done, leading to the next and the next until the story is over.

64

You're living inside the story, you're getting it out. It's just between you and your characters and you're old friends who don't care about grammar, spelling, and what mama will or won't allow around here.

Draft one is primal, like a scream, or a laugh or a sounding. It's your story in its rawest form. About the best you can say about it, is that it's done.

Some writers love draft one. They stay in it forever, or move on and write many, many "draft one" novels. I am happy for them if this makes them happy and keeps them off the street.

But they are amateurs, and their novels need to stay in their drawers or computers.

DRAFT 2: *Sense*

Your rough draft is what you want to say. Your subsequent drafts are how you want to say it.

Okay, now it's time to let another cherished person in: your reader.

Your book needs to make sense. It needs to be clear. It needs to be compelling. Your characters need to leap off the page with life.

My second drafts are multiple. I spend most of my writing time here.

In the second drafts it is vital to keep your reader in mind. Not how much you like this scene that brings to sparkling life your favorite coffee shop - but is it necessary to advance the plot?

Not how clever that turn of phrase is - but is it something that person would say?

Not showing off your research on the life of mid nineteenth century Choctaw people - but does it incorporate a detail that illuminates character?

Are there gaps in time, place, or character development? Are descriptions too sketchy or hackneyed?

Even when you think you've got a ship-shape chapter, pretend you must cut it by one fourth. Be merciless.

As Truman Capote famously said: "I believe more in the scissors than I do in the pencil."

DRAFT 3: *Sing*

Okay, story's out, and it makes sense. You've kept the pleasure of your reader in mind on every page. It is not full of gaps, nor is it overwritten, full of unnecessary scenes. It's clear, vital and compelling.

Now make it sing.

How? Read it aloud. If you run out of breath, the sentence is not right. If it sounds choppy or uneven, it is.

Are your transitions clear and smooth?

Do you mostly show, not tell and never preach?

Have you avoided clichés like the plague?

Look to your verbs. Are you using the best ones possible in every sentence?

How are the endings of each chapter? Do they compel your reader to turn the page?

Are your book's opening and closing scenes the absolute best they can be?

How about the opening and closing paragraphs?

And the first and last sentences?

Okay, it sings. And you're done.

*

It is perfectly okay to write garbage - as long as you edit brilliantly.

- C. J. Cherryh -

8

Transitions

Drama is life with the dull bits cut out. - **Alfred Hitchcock**

How do you get from Here to There?

Transitions pave the way from scene to scene. They are needed to provide change - of location, of point of view, of mood or tone, of time. They provide the narration that stitches your scenes together, without boring your reader. They come in many variations.

If your setting is new and important to establish fully, a transition might be a good place for description of place.

Breaks

Do you want your reader to go more seamlessly to the next scene? Perhaps only the time is changing? Then a paragraph and phrase might be all you need. This can be as simple as "Later that day ... " "As the night wore on ... " "Upon daybreak ... "

Need a little more of a break or the time frame is longer? Try a white space (triple space instead of double on your manuscript) to alert your reader that we're about to jump into another scene and/or viewpoint.

If it's a longer period of time still, maybe with a different scene and viewpoint, three asterisks separating the scenes may be in order.

The next bigger break is (or sometimes isn't) a chapter break. Perhaps you're going across the country or to another continent. Perhaps you're introducing a whole new character viewpoint - good reason for a chapter break.

Bending Transition Rules

But chapter breaks can also happen mid-scene as a tease - to get your reader to NOT turn off that light and go to bed! My wonderful editor at St. Martins Press, Natalia Aponte, was great at helping me find these spots, such as this one:

In *Waltzing in Ragtime*, Olana and Matt have traveled separate roads after a tumultuous three year romance and marriage, have met by chance on the streets of San Francisco after a long estrangement, and fall deliriously into bed together at Olana's place. Matt wakes up to Olana gone and a man serving him breakfast in bed. Olana chases the man (Basil) out but can't escape Matt's questions. She tells him that Basil brought breakfast to show he approves ...

> "Approves?"

> "Of us, Matthew."

> "Since when do we need your servant's approval?"

> "He's not my servant. He's my husband."

CHAPTER BREAK!

"No, he isn't."

"His name is Basil Edward - "

"You're married to me."

"Matthew, listen - "

"Did you divorce me? Did you burn sage and divorce me?"

"No."

"Then you're married to me, goddamn it!"

Anticipation

Anticipation's a good thing to encourage in your reader. So perhaps your transition might tease, give a taste of what will happen next. Foreshadow, with emotion.

"He'd promised to go to the party. But if she came, he didn't know if he could keep his temper in check."

Response

Good transitions can provide a response that will linger. Yes, even in transitions, your reader should have the sensation that she's getting all the good parts (see Alfred Hitchcock quote).

Clarity

Prime Directive of all transitions: Don't get your reader lost!

Exercises

1. Place. Look at one of your scenes with a new change of place. Write everything you know about this new place. Write your viewpoint character's feelings about this place. Write down how this place is important to your story. Does your transition illuminate both as well as move your story forward?

2. Work with a writing partner. Take a section of each other's novel. Look at transitions. Underline the transition words and phrases, highlight the breaks. Now: see if they work for you as a reader. Are they clear? Do they illuminate? Do they tease? Are they enough? Too much? Do they maintain or switch mood? Do they slow, maintain, or quicken the pace?

First edition, 1967.

9

Dialogue

Most writers like to use dialogue. What's not to like? Dialogue gets us out of our own muddled heads and into the characters' interaction with each other. "Researching" dialogue is eavesdropping. Looks nice on the page. Fills up those pages fast.

But ... is dialogue easy? No, it only appears that way. Dialogue in a novel is very different from real speech. Real speech is repetitive, boring and often inconclusive. Good dialogue is none of these things.

Good dialogue is the spine of your story. It gives your characters a chance to speak with their own voices, to converse with each other.

What stories do THEY have to tell? Dialogue illuminates their approach to others, their reactions to turns of the plot. It shows their speaking style, and how much they talk. They may use their own speech to communicate or to act as a barrier between themselves and others.

The Prime Directive of dialogue is to make it appear realistic while actually being finely crafted.

How is this accomplished?

Don't repeat in dialogue what has been explained in the narrative.

Too many dangling speeches are not intriguing. They will annoy and confuse.

Write your dialogue as tight as the rest of the novel - stay clear of long-winded soliloquies.

Don't use odd spellings to convey an accent or a speech impediment.

Avoid unnecessary dialogue tags ("hissed," "exclaimed peevishly"). "Said" works fine and paragraphing can be even better.

This is a finely crafted novel. You are not in bad-situation-comedy land. Avoid dialogue that is overly clever or silly.

Dialogue That Illuminates Character

My novel *The Randolph Legacy* is written in the limited third person viewpoints of its two main characters, Judith Mercer and Ethan Randolph. Ethan sees himself as small, misshapen and ugly. Judith is ruled by her Quaker upbringing to see only inner light. How to get a more objective viewpoint for my readers? I relied on a conversation Judith has with Mrs. Custis. To wit:

"We like your man. He's very handsome."

"I have always seen him so, but others, when he was sick, and with his lameness -"

"Lameness? What lameness, dear?"

"You did not notice?"

"Notice what?"

"Of course his boots help."

"Now, what woman with any eye for
beauty would be looking at the boots
of that fine formed man?"

In Robert Crooke's superb novel *The Earth and Its Sorrows*, his
protagonist's profession comes out in this dialogue with a
shopkeeper:

"It's funny. You don't act like
you're from here. You seem more like a
tourist."

"I guess I am, in a way." I
laughed. "But why -"

"You're friendly. I moved here from
New Jersey last year. Started my life
over, you might say." Her face held a
firm expression. "I lost my husband.
At the Trade Center."

"Oh no. I'm sorry."

She stared at me for a moment. "I keep wondering if I made a mistake."

"Moving here?"

"I like my new house. It's hard, though, making new friends. And this place, well, I don't know what I was thinking. It's not really an antique shop."

"It's unique," I said. "A pop-art museum."

"Yes," she agreed. "But people don't seem to get it. Maybe it's just me they don't get."

"People are generally nice, if you give them a chance."

She looked up briefly before finishing the sales slip.

"Have you advertised?" I suggested.

"I do a thing in the weekly shopper."

"You might encourage traffic with some events."

"What sort of events?"

"Cross-promotions with the bookstore up the street, for example. Have them display books from a certain era, and get a writer or historian to talk about the pop culture of that time. Tie it in to these objects you've got so people can see the context. Have some wine available."

She nodded. "People like wine. Are you in advertising?"

"Public relations. Retired now."

"I'll think about it," she said, pushing a nondescript shopping bag at me.

"Put your logo on these," I added.

How does dialogue advance the action of your story? Your story advances when characters argue, seduce, plan, give ultimatums, slight each other and gossip. (Remember those two women cackling over dead Scrooge's bed linens in *A Christmas Carol*?)

Each conversation should end with a condition being different. So check at the end of your dialogue scene: has the relationship altered? Has someone grown wiser? Do your speakers and readers now have some information they didn't have before?

Dialogue as Part of Voice

The attitude of the writer towards the story can be imbedded in dialogue. Think of the dialogue of Jane Austen's circumventing heroines, Janet Evanovich's Trenton babe, and Tony Hillerman's terse and incorruptible Navaho policemen.

Dynamic Dialogue

Good dialogue can show truth under pressure. How? By evasion, misunderstanding, exaggeration, lies. These keep the pressure on.

Speak the Speech

Make sure your dialogue has intensity. A few carefully honed words of dialogue can work better than paragraphs of explanation (the dreaded "tell"). Dialogue is character-specific. It moves your plot. It proclaims voice. Good dialogue has timing - it rings right in the ear. So go ahead and speak your written exchanges aloud. Remember Duke Ellington: "If it sounds good, it IS good!"

Exercises

1. Write a dialogue between two people: one has a secret, the other is trying to find out what it is.

2. Write a discussion between two people of different speaking styles - perhaps one is an upper class snob, the other proud of her

working class roots. Perhaps one has a non-native accent, and the other is prejudiced against foreigners. Perhaps the two speakers' moods are different - one is furious, the other is trying to calm her down.

3. Pick a character motivated by one force (greed, jealousy, envy, despair, hope, love, faith). Don't write the force but write, centered around that force:

      A.   a straight narrative

      B.   a dialogue

      C.   an action scene

4. Ask a character in your novel three questions. Answer them in your character's voice.

10

Show and Tell

Don't tell me the moon is shining, show me the glint of light on broken glass.

– Anton Checkhov

There are two ways to keep your story moving: showing and telling.

The pacing, the rhythm, the swing of your novel will be found in the decisions you make about when to show and when to tell.

Telling is just the facts. A whole novel written this way might be: A Kansas girl gets blown by a tornado to another place altogether. She has adventures that require wit, heart, and courage, before returning home.

Sometimes telling is all that's required to keep the story moving at a good clip. Those all important links, transitions, are usually in tell mode: "The next night ... " "A week of grueling twelve hour days later ... " "Seven years after the conviction ..."

But there are great opportunities to have the elements of your narrative do double and triple duty.

The reason you will hear "show don't tell!" invoked is because showing engages the reader more - emotionally and on a sensory level.

Showing can illuminate character.

The prisoner of war awaited punishment. That tells what's going on in this section of *The Randolph Legacy*. But who is he?

```
His eyes darted everywhere. A salt sea
wind blew across the deck, sending his
dark hair out of its neat queue and
into his powder-burned face. The soles
of his feet were bleeding, as if
they'd never been toughened by deck
work or climbing rigging. And his legs
```

were pale below his breeches. When the
boy's short blue jacket was pulled
off, another puzzle: the shirt beneath
it was beautiful. Its generous yardage
billowed in the breeze, adding a touch
of grace to the grim occasion.

Showing can help bring your setting to life. A country-bred man sat
in his San Francisco garden in *Waltzing in Ragtime*:

The early morning fog hung tight and
low. In the distance, he heard cable
cars starting down Market Street. In
an hour he'd be on one, heading for
his small office on the outskirts of
Chinatown. He'd carefully cultivated
this ground and through its bounty
found seasons. The fragrant Tamarack
pine he'd planted when they'd first
come was now taller than Possom. He
ran his finger along its dark green
bundle of needles. Along the trellis
he'd built for them, yellow roses

```
opened. There had to be something
redeeming about a place where roses
bloomed in January.
```

Showing can make action elements more effective.

Tell your story in the opposite rhythm of real life.

Is that trip to the mountain cabin long and uneventful? Just tell us that and get on with it!

Is a hungry wolf going for your father's throat? Borrow a technique from Japanese Kabuki theatre and slow way down so that your readers can enjoy the tension and excitement.

From *In the Time of the Wolves*:

```
Daddy answered the wolf's growl with a
murmur in a language I didn't
understand. His arm reached behind his
back where his weapon was slung. As
his hand touched cold iron, the wolf
sprung.
```

"Stay back!" he commanded me or the wolf or perhaps us both.

But for me to obey him, meant to let him die.

My father took the force of the attack squarely. I heard the sickening sound of his head hitting the balsam's protruding roots. The strong hands I'd known my life long were now lost in glistening fur as he struggled to keep the wolf from his throat. His pulse pounded in his neck, so exposed, so fragile.

Showing can expand the power of the element of dialogue.

A lawyer and his daughter engage a cabman's services in a rough dockside neighborhood of New York City, 1851.

From *Honor to the Hills:*

"We wish to retain your services for the length of our visit aboard The Atlantic Sovereign." My father pulled a crisp new note of currency from his wallet. "Will this suffice?"

The cabman's eyes went wide. "Oh, nicely, sir."

"Thank you." Daddy held out his hand.

The cabman hesitated, then swiped his own fingerless gloved hand across his vest and took it. "You ain't from around here, are you, Squire?"

My father winced at the honorific, then smiled. "We're from upriver. Does it show?"

"Mightily!"

Showing in real time can trigger a character's memory and send your narrative into flashback. There is a danger that this will slow down your forward movement or cause confusion, but if done well, it will be accepted as essential.

Here is a World War II Navajo code-talker breaking the taboo of his culture to bury a fellow serviceman in *The Airman's Wife*:

He was a poor choice for this. The
airman deserved one of his own. Never
mind. Keep digging, Luke told himself,
deep enough that the remains will not
be disturbed.

He had to step into the hole. Fear
stung the roots of his hair. Stop it.
Keep digging.

Luke remembered the spirit song of a
chain gang of prison workers he'd
passed on the streets of Flagstaff
once -- a beautiful, tormented chant,
looking for a long-gone mother,
father, sister, brother. But a song
that ended in light. Luke had tried to
replicate the music on his flute.

Suddenly its melody, complete with the ending words came into his mind --

Bright morning star arising

Day is a breakin' in my soul

Luke sang out the song.

The wind answered, whipping around him, swaddling the body of the airman tighter in his parachute.

Luke climbed out of the grave, pulled off his watch cap, and faced the one who had been Philippe Charente. Squarely, not out of a corner of his sight as he had been doing since the man's last breath.

Finish. He was a soldier now. Perhaps this would be the first of many he'd be called upon to bury.

Both your novel as a whole and every part of your novel has a beginning, a middle and an end. That's where you'll find your story's pace, its swing. So dissect the whole, each scene, each paragraph, each sentence, and even the sound of each word to make sure it all fits. And to find where your pacing is off.

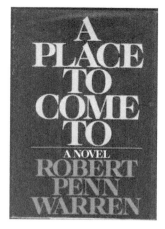

First edition, 1977.

Exercises

1. Go through your novel as if you're going to turn it into a movie. Label each scene by its setting, day or night, interior or exterior, characters. Step back and evaluate how varied the scenes are.

2. Speed up a non-action scene.

3. Slow down an action scene.

First edition, 1960.

II

To Prologue or Epilogue?

Do prologues and epilogues seem hopelessly quaint? Not at all.
Some novels call out for one, the other, or both. Some are fine
without. In foodie terms, I think of the prologue as an appetizer,
the epilogue, like that piece of chocolate on your reader's pillow.

Prime Directives of prologues and epilogues: Make them necessary;
make them brief.

Prologues and epilogues usually cover a time period not within the
confines of your story. They should contribute to the book,
enhance the reader's understanding and pleasure in ways that can't
be done within the novel's main confines.

Why Prologue?

Many times a prologue provides a crucial part of the novel's back story. In a science fiction or historical novel, this may be background material - world building. In a mystery, it may be a character sitting on death row thinking back to how he got in all this trouble to begin with.

It's the first thing your reader lays eyes on, so it better be a compelling hook. But is it only that? Perhaps you need to cut it out and make your first chapter more compelling.

Some prologues just lift a scene from the middle of the book. Why? Because it's exciting? That's not enough of a reason.

In my novels *Waltzing in Ragtime*, *Rachel LeMoyne* and *The Randolph Legacy*, I illuminated a pivotal incident in a character's past . Both Matthew Hart and Ethan Randolph start their stories with much hidden. I wanted to let the reader in on the moments of their lives that led to where they are at their stories' beginnings.

Rachel LeMoyne's journey starts with a prologue covering the Choctaw ceremony of saying goodbye to their trees before the journey west on their Trail of Tears. Rachel's book continues her travels, always in the company of trees, right to the epilogue, when she gives birth under a tree's sheltering branches.

In *The Ghosts of Stony Clove*, my first person narrator tells the reader that she is about to tell her own version of the story of her coming of age before it becomes a tall tale of the Catskill Mountains.

Why Epilogue?

Like the prologue, the epilogue is used for dramatic effect. That's why my *Waltzing in Ragtime* doesn't have one. Even I didn't dare compete with the San Francisco Earthquake for dramatic effect.

Epilogues are popular in Romance novels, where many readers are fond of learning a bit of the "how" of their couple's happy ever after. Had Jane Austen but indulged in epilogues, perhaps we wouldn't be suffering the current deluge of bad sequels to *Pride and Prejudice*.

Epilogues are also used by novelists who want to pull you into the next book of a series. Crafty! A taste of what happens next! When I wrote the epilogue for *The Ghosts of Stony Clove*, I had no such intention, but my young readers, once they'd read Ginny finish her story as she's feeling the first pangs of her birthing labor, demanded to know what happened next. I was very happy they did, as a three generation series was born as a result of their prodding.

Exercise

Gather up and examine the prologues and epilogues of several current novels. Do they work? How do they work? On how many levels? Compare them to your own. Do yours work as well?

First edition, 1989.

12

Market!

It is impossible to discourage real writers - they don't give a damn what you say, they're going to write. - **Sinclair Lewis**

The moment you give all or any portion of your novel to someone else to read, you are engaged in marketing. Call it "feedback" call it, "honey, does this scene make sense to you?" call it, "Mom, be kind!" - you are engaged in selling! So let's get the prime directive out of the way:

Prime Directive of Criticism: No matter what anyone says about anything you write, it is saying more about that person than it is saying about your work.

That's why writers are often urged to get into critique groups with other writers - because people who love us are usually not the best sources for objective judgment.

Save your sensitive soul for the process of writing your novel. Work had to develop a thick, thick skin when you're ready to put it out in the world.

Because, unless you're in the rarified world of genius (that would be the known-by-one-names ... Shakespeare, Mozart, Einstein, Cher) you're going to have to go through a few or a boatload of NO before you get to a YES. And you have to survive to get to those *yes* people and cherish them forever. The way there? Reread the Prime Directive!

Connecting: Writers Groups

You may choose to not market any draft of your novel to anyone until it gets to an editor's desk. That's perfectly valid.

But, if you choose to seek feedback while the novel is being written, I'd suggest readers you trust. I have had the great pleasure and privilege to belong to many writers groups. Some have worked better than others. All have been helpful.

Even before anyone uttered a word, the process of hearing my work being read aloud was beneficial because, remember Duke Ellington: *If it sounds good, it is good.*

In a working writers group, each participant knows it will be her work's turn during the course of the session. That usually does wonders for social skills like being considerate and trying to say something nice or encouraging before the boom is lowered. Please try to be one of those people who are sensitive to fellow writers. For encounters with those without filters ... please refer yourself, again, to the Prime Directive.

People in writers groups usually have different tastes in reading. You will have a good idea about the reading taste of your compatriot through her own work. Good writing is good writing, but I love a critique partner who reads a lot from a lot of genres, because I'm looking for a wide readership for my work. I read many genres, with the exception of Horror. When I have a Horror manuscript to critique, I make that clear to the writer, so she can take my ignorance into consideration. I enjoy reading Romance, so when I observe that a heroine is of the too-stupid-to-live variety that readers of the genre complain about, or a hero who is cruel to women, children or animals (a no-no within the conventions of the genre), I try to point these things out.

Take What You Need, Leave the Rest

Don't stay in a group that doesn't leave you feeling energized and eager to move your work forward.

Success Story

When she joined our writers group, Romance novelist Jenna Kernan had a strong desire, loved her research and her stories and characters, and an open heart. She was also an astute and considerate reader. Jenna did not have her elements of the novel in firm grasp. She took notes, asked questions for clarification and was incredibly diligent and hard working. She is now a successful multi-published author whose novels grow richer and more compelling each year. We are so proud of her!

Post Publication

After your novel is published and out in the wide, wide world, the Prime Directive also holds true. You can take critics as: had-a-bad-day, narrow-minded trolls (those who write bad reviews) or brilliant astute and insightful (those who write glowing reviews of your novel). But the fact is, there are creative writers and there are creative readers, and you hope your novel gets one of the latter as reviewer. I have had reviewers write reactions that steal my breath and warm my soul. Their perception brings grace and beauty to my work.

But no matter how bad or good the review, the Prime Directive holds true. I treasure all readers who take the time and trouble to articulate their appreciation of my stories, because in doing so they become advocates of the work of my heart.

First edition, 1993.

Scotland Forever

For those days when the critics are on your trail, here's the supreme answer to a bad review from the Robert Burns playbook. Feel free to borrow any or all to hurl like thunderbolts at your oppressor. Who knew Robert Burns could remind one of Yosemite Sam, if you get him mad enough??

Ellisland, 1791.

Dear Sir:

Thou eunuch of language; thou Englishman, who never was south the Tweed; thou servile echo of fashionable barbarisms; thou quack, vending the nostrums of empirical elocution; thou marriage-maker between vowels and consonants, on the Gretna-green of caprice; thou cobler, botching the flimsy socks of bombast oratory; thou blacksmith, hammering the rivets of absurdity; thou butcher, embruing thy hands in the bowels of orthography; thou arch-heretic in pronunciation; thou pitch-pipe of affected emphasis; thou carpenter, mortising the awkward joints of jarring sentences; thou squeaking dissonance of cadence; thou pimp of gender; thou Lyon Herald to silly etymology; thou antipode of grammar; thou executioner of construction; thou brood of the speech-distracting builders of the Tower of Babel; thou lingual confusion worse confounded; thou scape-gallows from the land of syntax; thou scavenger of mood and tense; thou murderous accoucheur of infant learning; thou ignis fatuus, misleading the steps of benighted ignorance; thou pickle-herring in the puppet-show of nonsense; thou faithful recorder of barbarous idiom; thou persecutor of syllabication; thou baleful meteor, foretelling and facilitating the rapid approach of Nox and Erebus.

R.B.

Connecting: Professional Organizations

Writers associations provide many benefits for members, including newsletters, competitions, media mailings, networking, writing resources and support. There is, of course, a cost involved with these benefits, so investigate carefully to see what association(s) - if any - best suit your needs.

American Christian Fiction Writers: *acfw.com*

American Crime Writers League: *acwl.org*

The Authors Guild: *authorsguild.org*

Electronic Literature Association: *eliterature.org*

EPIC: The Electronic Publishing Industry Coalition: *epicorg.com*

Historical Novel Society: *historicalnovelsociety.org*

Horror Writers Association: *Horror.org*

Military Writers Society of America: *militarywriters.com*

National Writers Association: *nationalwriters.com*

National Writers Union: *nwu.org*

Novelists, Inc.: *ninc.com*

Romance Writers of America: *rwa.org*

Science Fiction and Fantasy Writers of America: *sfwa.org*

Sisters in Crime: *sistersincrime.org*

Small Publishers, Writers, and Artists Network: *spawn.org*

Society of Children's Book Writers and Illustrators: *scbwi.org*

Western Writers of America: *westernwriters.org*

Women Writing the West: *womenwritingthewest.org*

Afterword

Our greatest glory is not in never failing but in rising up each time we fail.

- Ralph Waldo Emerson

The Business

Writing a novel is a craft, an art, and a business. If you write, you're a writer. If you complete a novel, you're a novelist. If you're engaged in finding a paying audience of readers, you're in business. As a business person you are under the obligation to teach yourself about the business and keep up with its changing realities.

How? Subscribe to professional magazines and websites. Join professional organizations that fit the genre of novel you write. Visit the websites of publishers who are the home of your favorite authors. Enter contests. Put your social mask on. Go to conferences. Meet fellow novelists (and editors and agents). If you do these things often enough, you'll get the hang of it, and may click with some who will become lifelong friends and advocates.

Don't do these things so much that your writing suffers. You must provide plenty of product to sell.

Support Etiquette

Along the way of your journey towards crafting your novels, you will meet many wonderful fellow travelers who will provide support, encouragement, teaching - at a book-signing, a talk, a writer's conference, a class. Please buy their books for yourself or as gifts. If you enjoy their novels, please review them, please encourage others to buy them. It's good manners. And your kind generosity will be remembered.

The Final Prime Directives ...

They are six:

1. Engage your reader from the first to the last sentence. (Thou shalt not bore the reader!)

2. Don't confuse or let your story wander aimlessly.

3. Make your characters memorable and life-like.

4. Make your scenes vivid and compelling.

5. Don't forget that not every reader is your reader.

6. Disregard 1-5 if necessary.

About Number 6 ...

As W. Somerset Maugham observed: "There are three rules for writing the novel. Unfortunately, no one knows what they are."

This guide has been prescriptive, but, I hope, not rule heavy. Rules tend to become a straight jacket, and that's the last thing we want in fiction. So number six is your permission to break any or all rules in the process of getting your story out. Show your poetic license and proceed!

Getting good at this may take some time. So, dear novelist, take care of yourself. Eat well, and not too much. Stay clear of all drugs including tobacco and too much alcohol. Exercise regularly. Enjoy your friends and family. Participate in your community and the natural and cultural worlds it contains. Be good to them all, and to yourself. Yours is a calling to beautify the earth with story.

Make it so!

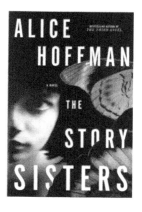

First edition, 2009.

Acknowledgments

Profound thanks to all my fellow writers and editors who have been my teachers.

Some of them: Bill and Diana Gleasner, Alicia Rasley, Paula Graves, Janet S. Corcoran, Robert Crooke, Tony Hillerman, Juilene Osborne McKnight, Robert J. Sawyer, Meredith Sue Willis, Edward Renehan, Kathryn Erskine, Russell C. Jones, Jody Hedlund, Janet Evanovich, Harry McLeod, Beth Hill, Vicki Britton, Alice Hoffman, Marg McAlister, Sara Furlong-Burr, Jenna Kernan, Mac Nelson, Diane Michele Crawford, Jim Green, Elise Donner, Sandra Jordan, Natalia Aponte, Barry Holstun Lopez, Dee Oiler, Margie Rhoadhouse, Patrica A. Rodgers, Susan Shackleford, Barbara Ward Lazarsky, Walter Gobel, Laurie Maxwell, Carolyn Bennett, Paul Healy, Charlie Rineheimer, Mitze Flyte, Susan King, Deborah Barnhart, Christine Whittemore, Meredith Bean McMath, Nicholas W. Quick, Eileen Nauman, Kathleen Dehler, Rose Eichhorn, Betsy Tunis, Jonathan Schmidt, Cathy Rockwell, Yvonne Yirka.

About the Author

EILEEN CHARBONNEAU'S historical novels for adults include *Waltzing in Ragtime, The Randolph Legacy* and *Rachel LeMoyne*, all published by Macmillan/Forge. *The Washington Post* said of *Waltzing in Ragtime* that it "has an almost made-for-TV miniseries sheen to it, even as it grapples with large and complex social issues ... " Charbonneau's YA novels include *The Ghosts of Stony Clove, In the Time of the Wolves* and *Honor to the Hills*, all published by Macmillan/Tor. Charbonneau has also written for *The New York Times* and co-wrote the award-winning 1990 documentary film *Endowment for the Planet*, narrated by Christopher Reeve. She lives in Maplecrest, New York and Boca Raton, Florida.

Photo: Fyodor A. Pavlov.

About the Publisher

New Street Communications, LLC, publishes and distributes superior works of nonfiction (and, through our Dark Hall Press imprint, select fiction in the Horror genre). We are a *digital-native* imprint. As such, we primarily make our titles available as eBooks, though often in paper editions as well.

On the nonfiction side of things, we cover the intersection of digital technology and society; transformative business communication and innovation (particularly the conceptualizing of elegant new tools, markets, products and paradigms); socially-relevant children's literature; and literary criticism. New Street's nonfiction books are authored by distinguished scholars, journalists, entrepreneurs, developers and thought leaders.

newstreetcommunications.com

Made in the USA
Middletown, DE
31 July 2023